SEASON

of

POEMS

Kimberly Dorough

Fulton Books
Meadville, PA

Published by Fulton Books 2023

ISBN 979-8-88731-689-5 (paperback)
ISBN 979-8-88731-690-1 (digital)

Printed in the United States of America

I'd like to dedicate this book of Poems to my beautiful children Joshua and Alyssa. They have been my driving force and greatest love of all. They are true examples for others in their path, and continue to impress and make all of us proud. Love you, Josh and Alyssa!

When Does Life Get Good?

When I look at my Nemo with wondering eyes
And see the all beauty that within him lies.

When I see a baby in a stroller smiling,
I look through his smile and start sighing.

When does life get good?

When the sun rises in the east, painting it reminds me,
That another day is on the horizon, ready to meet thee.

For goodness' sake, when the trees turn orange and red,
And this fall when I get to tuck myself early to bed.

When the day is long but productive,
And the wind outside is seductive.

When does life get good?

When all I can think of is my children at work,
And when I get home to kiss and hug them and they not shirk.

When all seems lost but my husband is still there,
To comfort me and show me that he really does care.
When does life get good?

When aunts and uncles come calling,
And cousins are dawning.

When I know in my heart everything is going to be okay,
Even when the heartbreak lasts all day.

When my mom and dad call me on the phone,
And say I love you! Come home!

When does life get good?

When every day that passes I'm still here,
Planning, organizing, loving, feeling, listening, without fear.

When the piano, flute, and trumpet toll,
And music fills my soul.

When does life get good?

I can think of when life gets good,
When family and friends stay under hood.

I thank thee for all that is good.
And in that moment everything in all the world be could.

When the Bluebirds Sing

When the bluebirds sing,
My heart starts to ring,
It's on the way, spring,
The bells toll *ding-a-ling*.

I can't say enough about the flowers,
They look like they have so much power,
Roses, daffodils, pansies, marigolds,
Beauty unforetold.

Spring has a way of changing everything,
Making it all right, bluebirds catch wing,
The trees, and sky, the breeze,
What a tease.

See into my heart bluebirds start,
Sing with praise, play the part,
Seeds of plenty,
I try to be friendly.

They reach up, up, up,
Yet I can see them close-up,
Spring has such a fine atmosphere,
It is that that I'm well aware.

Easter is on the way,
Bluebirds sing in their hay day,
May all the wonders that may,
Appease you today.

Summer

You start out so beautiful,
then I feel the pull,
to go to the beach, take in the sun,
Wash away my cares, all at once.

Thank you, Summer, for giving us so much!
The rest of the year long,
I long to touch,
So many vacation plans,
and so many opportunities for tans.

Yet work is still a troublesome factor,
to get out of it, yes, that's the matter,
Oh, Summer! Please stay awhile,
till I can see the shadow on the sundial.

And that I can still make a sand castle,
just some sand molded into a pile,
Wait, run into the ocean and feel,
The sun on my back, hopefully it does not peel.

Summer, romantically and nostalgically, you are the one
the one to lie there unapologetically
and hope people get their time in
Into June, July, and August.

Light

You blind me
Yet your all-encompassing
Light, what do you do to me
Except heal me

I cannot express my thanks
Light, you are there for me
And brighten my way
That I might stay in your warmth

Please give me a path
That I may take
Help me
Find my way

Light, be there all my days
To expand my eyes
And brighten my horizons
Come to me, Light

The Orlando Temple

The Orlando Temple sits on a hill,
Lights up at night and I look until,
Alas, I am prompted to go inside,
It is then that I am filled with pride.

To do the work for the dead,
Yes, that's what I said,
Endowments, sealings, baptisms, and initiatories,
That's the story.

Don't give up, get a temple recommend
Then you'll see,
What can truly come to be?
The most beautiful service to thee.

The Orlando Temple is lit up at night,
I try to go there all the days of my life,
I try and try with all my might,
My timetable is always so tight!

Try as I may,
I might as well stay,
Longer, and longer each time,
Filling my heart with rhyme.

Winter

Winter, the cold blistery snow,
Oh, how cold,
No one knows until you're really there,
In the thick of it, fluffy, white, bare.

Clean, brisk, and feeling numb,
The evergreens, I try my green thumb,
They say you are so pretty,
And yet so insignificantly petty.

But as a whole, you snow,
I love you so,
You take the dirt away,
And lead me astray.

Into the wind, where I am scared yet mesmerized,
To be here now I know it must be sanctified.
Winter, you don't disappoint,
What a positively wonderful joint.

And yet still my child has not seen you!

Heaven

The Pearly White Gates
The Streets of Gold
The flowers of every color, tastes
Of things unforetold.

The forever after
Into the eternities unfold
The bright white light
That engulfs you with love.

Are you really there, Jesus?
To meet me and hug?
That my bones might melt
In this warmth I've not known, tug.

That I am forever changed
From the chains of death
And that I might see more clearly
Than through the pains of earth.

You are there I know
I've been told since I was eight.
It's going to be great,
When we meet at Heaven's Gate.

The Invisible Enemy

A beautiful sunflower blooms in the moonlight.

We sit on a log watching the fire crackle at a campsite.

Hand sanitizer, antibacterial soap, toilet paper, and
disinfectant wipes gone with not a hope for more in the
near future even in this day in age being ever so slight.

When will we understand and win this war we fight?

How long will we have to bear this COVID-19 plight?

When we are challenged to the brink and see an end in sight?

Thank you to those selfless service providers including teachers,
nurses, and doctors, who tirelessly care about us and our children
and their patients, who are holding all of us together tight!

How can we thank those health-care providers and
mask and ventilator makers with all our might?

Save your tears for those we have lost this
year and last to this virus, this night.

Let bygones be bygones and hug those you love stronger
than the wind fluttering against a flying kite.

So here we are holding it together for our children, family and
friends, jobs, and our country with the hope of a new day we
so desperately want to arrive but may be somewhat trite.

Keep your spirits high, help your neighbors in need, but
stay home, unless, indeed, but spare no love or compassion
on those whom you know will benefit at this time, who

may be the person standing six feet in front of you or six
feet behind. Take heart and know this will come to an end,
and until then allow your invisible wings to take flight.

Thank those who have come to the rescue: the doctors, nurses,
paramedics, EMS, hospitals, and ambulances to be polite.

We are grateful for the media, the government, the president, the
researchers and scientists, the grocery store workers, the banks, the
restaurants, the gas stations, sanitation workers, mail carriers, and
truck drivers, working around the clock and into the twilight.

Through all the financial turmoil, blatant confusion, and uncertain
future at this time, let us press onward and ride it out like a knight.

This coronavirus has claimed so many lives, family, friends,
and people we know and love across the globe. This ravaging
contagion has traveled far and wide from the Orient
and beyond, only to come down with a nasty bite.

This pandemic outdoes 1918. However. it cannot take our peace,
even through isolation, social distancing, and quarantine.

Take a knee for New York, New Jersey, Michigan,
and Louisiana, classified as our hot spot sites.

For those who have lost their jobs, or income, we feel your pain, our
hearts swell with kindness and service that at this time shines bright.

Let's keep the music in our hearts, like a tiny little sprite.

Let us help each other, as we know to do,
as that would only be right.

With all of our souls combined, we plead, "Let this wash
away forever," down the drain with a bottle of Woolite.

The sustenance we seek comes from above through those
who are inspired and able to hear that still small voice,
in turn leaving us totally and completely contrite.

Let us look up and pray for relief from this
madness to reach a greater height.

Hope to our heavenly Father we don't stand
alone, but join the cavalry and suffer no more,
but soar above the fluffy clouds of white.

We are calling on angels to lift us out of this morbid sight.

Trust in the Lord and we shall see the light.

Moon and Stars

Where are you, Moon and Stars?
Way off in the distance afar,
Light years away,
Takes more than a day.

You brighten up the midnight sky,
Flecks of paradise.
Moon and Stars, there you are,
Come out tonight on par.

The light you shineth,
Makes my dreams the finest.
Shooting star, make my dreams come true,
And Man in the Moon, you too!

Stars, tell me something,
Will you be out nightly?
I know you're predictable,
But oh so magical.

Moon and Stars, come meet me tonight on my porch,
That I might rock in my rocking chair once more.
Moon and Stars, you are so bright,
Take me away tonight.

My Child

My Child, You Are a Gift from God

You are my truest and most wonderful blessing of all,
You give life to my soul!

You are the reason I live,
You have so much to give!

You give life to everything around,
Your sweet spirit makes everything sound.

The beauty in your eyes,
And yet you're still mine!

Please keep being you!
And then we will see through.

The wondering heart of a child,
You make me feel so mild.

The innocence of your face,
What grace.
You cannot be replaced!

My Son

You take my breath away,
with your genius mind, don't let it lead you astray.

My son, what you have done already seems daunting,
and your tasks that lie in front of you don't seem haunting.

You give and give of yourself,
to have as our own is our true wealth.

You take my heart with you wherever you go,
Take my love, soul, and smile in tow.

You are my greatest accomplishment,
and yet you leave me in astonishment.

How can you be so talented, so smart?
With all of us with you, you play the part!

Son, don't change,
Stay the same.

Christmastime

Christmastime!
You brighten up everyone's spirit.
Especially mine,
We look around and come for it.

Please don't say I am going to have to spend a lot of money,
Someone, please come rescue me.
For money isn't grown on trees.
Things aren't free.

But there is a sweet spot,
In our hearts.
Of the birth of Jesus,
He plays the part.

Take heed, He comes quickly,
When you least expect it.
It might feel prickly,
But you need to accept it.

Christmastime, please be kind,
To me and all my friends.
Thank you for the time,
That seems to never end!

Yet it will come to a stop,
Once the New Year is upon us.
Make your fun, exciting, glow pop,
So next year we won't have a fuss.

Christmastime, thank you again.
To all those who are cheerful and jolly.
For all the magic and inspiration,
Full of mistletoe and holly.

Loving Never Fails

Loving never fails,
Loving from a distance
Loving from up close
Yeah, it makes a world of difference
Even when it is bespoke

Yeah, loving never fails
It always tells a tale
With you here by my side
I take it all in pride
Someone I have with me all the time
Makes my heart sing with rhyme

Loving never fails
It's richer every day
The more I feel I pray
That you will not leave
But please stay!

Come with me downtown
And we can get together
You and me forever
Loving never fails

With it comes great tales
And I can see in the distance
That this love is the difference
Take it all in pride
With you by my side

Memories

Next time you have a memory jot it down,
Because it'll help you remember the little things.
The things that come up so quickly.
Otherwise forget it, you will frown.

Memories, touch me deep within
Sideways, upways, ever so thin.
Like a smooth tall glass
Ringing the rim.

I remember you, memories!
Some are bad and some are good.
Please help me remember the fantasies!
Before thee stood.

Pain

You most sour thing!
You put me to the test,
And still make it rain.
Tell me what?
Have I done something in vain?

Please tell me why do I deserve this?
It doesn't go away.
Please leave me a gentle kiss.
Don't make it stay.

Pain, you have corrupted me,
Taken my joy with you.
Somehow I must get it back,
Or else you will have won too!

Please release me, Pain!
Please forgive me!
I do not stare at you this way!
And only then will I be complete,
When the pain is gone
And I can sing with song.
And retreat.

The Need for Speed

I get into my red Ford Mustang convertible,
Cruise down the road a tangle.
The wind in my hair,
And top down if I dare!

Feeling so good,
With the music blaring,
Speeding like I ever could,
Singing without caring!

I have the need for speed,
Yes, all the girl inside of me.
You know me to a tee,
Yet not so fast, I know thee.

I have the key that starts this engine,
EcoBoost, you say,
That's my ignition!
That's why I pray.

Well, hitting the road with my tires skidding,
I don't freak out! Are you kidding!

Smooth sailing from here on out,
Not a care in the world to fret about!

Southern Charm

Isn't it nice, a big glass of water and ice?
On a hot summer day in the south?

Don't take my word to suffice!
Let it melt in your mouth.

The southern charm is all so nice,
When breezy wind and sunsets entice.

What more could you want?
Than to see the palm trees flaunt.

Anyway, in the south, it's warm all right,
But all that company?
Oh no, not a fright.
For it is a welcome party!

Food

Spaghetti and meatballs, yum,
Pizza and eggrolls, in my tum.

Seafood, what a splendor,
Food, I am your big spender.

Food, you warm my heart and soul,
I truly live when I have a soup bowl.

Hot tamales, and empanadas!
Green tomatoes, and peppers, aha!

Food, you are a pleasure,
To do business with you, what a measure!

Yum, yum, yum,
I love you, food, and where are you from?

Take me there away if you dare,
Food always has a way to stare.

Right through me, peanut butter and celery,
Apple pie and cheese.

Oh, when is it enough!
Brisket, mac and cheese, and baked beans?
Food, you most delight,
And aid in my plight!

Cakes, cookies, and candy!
Who brought the party?

The most fun yet,
Sprinkles, buttercream, and fondant,
When did we become despondent?

Because whenever you're around,
There I might be found!

Love

Oh, it's all right, or maybe I uptight?
Love, does it make everything right?

Love, can you be the answer,
To life's questions or are you a cancer?

Love, when will I see you?
Is it when I am asked to be married?
Or when I'm on my first date?
Love, will you be my fate?

I love you, *Love*
I know you must come from above!

Love, it sure is fleeting.
But then again, what are we beating?

Is it a lifelong problem?
Or does love solve it?

Love, can you please come to my rescue?
Otherwise I don't know what I'll pursue!

Love, you bring out the best in me!
And then I can really see.

The life you love have given me.
Love, you are my destiny!

He Comes Again!

He comes in a white robe and burgundy sash,
He is not here to throw a lash!

On a white stallion horse,
why it's his steed of course!

Angels will be singing and praising His name,
till we're all called home again the same.

Let glory be to God,
Jesus says with a nod.

From on high He arrives,
don't all run and hide!

The misty morning adieu,
for alas His light comes through.

Well, we will see,
there is no guarantee,

that we'll be saved,
from our iniquities.

Yet He did die on the cross for us,
you can only hope it's true.

That we will see Him again,
through thick or thin!

Devotedly loyal constantly,
I know He'll come for me inherently.

House for Sale

Oh, house for sale,
I see you and want you, oh my!
What can it be in pale?
That I just sigh!

Oh, house for sale,
Every floor, porch, lanai,
Comes into my heart and without fail,
I'll buy you, of course, for I do see not why.

Come to my open house you say!
I will eat the cookies and stay!

The bathrooms, bedrooms, and stairs,
They are all my taste in fair.

I saw that sign on the road,
"House for Sale"
Please don't be too expensive for me to afford.
So we all can live there on one accord!

Sadness

Why do you come to me, sadness, so?
I can hardly carry the load.

Sadness, you really are there, aren't you?
To make us all feel low and woe me, too.

Depression, tears, cries out in fear.
Sadness, please let go from me, oh dear.

Or I will succumb,
With unwavering yield.

Oh, please leave me, sadness,
Or salvage the mess!

Cozy on the Couch

Cozy on the couch, I might as well be,
If you're watching a movie, that'll be me.

Come here and get close,
On the couch with me!

Don't you see this could be the start?
Of the very satisfying part!

Where not only holding hands,
Is all that happens?

But communicating in ways,
I could not begin to understand.

Yes, cozy on the couch with thee,
Surely it is for me.

Whether we're talking, reading, or laughing,
We're just being!

Close and cozy on the couch!

Marriage

Marriage, yes, they say it is hard.
Like walking through a bucket full of lard.

Yet it can be sweet,
And homey, a great retreat.

From earthly cares,
That of course thin they wear.

Marriage, it is sewn out of love,
Angels sing from above.

When will you realize that it surely is of God?

That we get to spend the rest of our lives,
With someone with whom we trod.

Writing

Writing, it lifts my spirit,
And I am filled with lyrics.

Writing calms my soul,
When life really takes a toll.

When will it all come down on me?
When I am down and out,
Will writing leave me stout?

Someone once told me,
Writing brings out your feelings,
That made it seem quite appealing.

How can we see through someone's writing?
If we're not trying!
Writing, it surely is cathartic,
That's why people do it!

Writing, you have my attention!
Yet it is difficult for it to come to fruition.
Writing, you see me for as I am,
And won't judge me, like I have been.

Can you take away my sorrows?
And help me live for my tomorrows?

Writing, please let my words out,
That I might be better, all around.

Writing, you are astute,
When I think, you come to the acute,
Stage at which I am in,
The stage that I need.

The words indeed,
Help me win!

Follow Me 2023

What can I say but follow me,
This year will be like no other.

'Cause I am truly your mother,
Follow me, into the light,
And you will see,
Your life will be bright!

Follow me, that's what they say,
When you're an example, and in the day,
When you're afraid,
Follow me, and stay by my side.

Oh, you must follow me,
Because all I've done for you,
Surely it's true,
I have been put on a pedestal.

When you see me, you'll know
The sunshine is coming!
If only you follow me,
You could make big money!

Follow me, and it'll be quite crazy, but
Life goes on in the hazy,
Storms we share,
Why not give a care?

And follow me,
Into the sea,
Where it is calm, beautiful, and serene,
What a wonderful scene!

I can see it now,
Following me, how?
But you can do it!
I have faith in you through it!

What I cannot tell you is what to do,
But if you listen,
Somehow you'll get through.

When we oft seem apart,
Come follow me, and play the part.
Take your time,
And you'll see life, into mine.

Take heed, it will be tough,
Harder than hard,
Yes, it is rough!

But I've had a great life!
If only you follow me,
To a tee,
There will be no more strife.

What more can I say
Than obey!
Follow me and you'll see,
Come what may!

Touch

I believe in the human touch!
Not too close but hugs a much!

The hands clasped together,
Any storm they can weather.

Pianos play in the distance,
And we sway,
Into the arms, of the ones we love
A gift from above.

The human touch, it feels
Fingerprints wit will wield.

Thank heavens for touch,
Maybe we should have lunch?

Take me in your arms, and say
I love you, in so many ways.

Hugs a plenty,
May the world never end a many.

Days in the life of touch, and the senses,
What more can we ask for than perspective?

Touch it goes right through you,
Like a warm blanket too!

Touch, will you always stay?
Keep the bad feelings away.

Touch, the guardian of my heart,
May the tides that be protect it?
From the heavens to the earth,
Touch, come to birth!

Chocolate

Oh my gosh, Chocolate, you complete me!
So soft and oh so creamy!

Dark chocolate, and ones with nuts,
No, I'm not crazy, just kaput!

All in a tizzy for chocolate,
My archenemy,

However, it really is so dreamy!
Chocolate, there are many factories,

Cocoa, milk chocolate, Hershey's Kisses,
All the chocolate wishes!

Combine into my senses,
Chocolate, make some messes,

With baking Nestle chocolate chips,
Into cookies you come to be!

So sweet and savory, the hips,
Of these wonderful concoctions we see!

Towers, and chocolate monuments,
Chocolate-covered strawberries, and chocolate mints!

Oh, my love for chocolate,
Let me put you in my pocket!

Don't eat too much though,
Because you'll get sick!

Ha ha, I know, right,
Quick!
Oh, but it is so good,

Can't get enough,
Of chocolate,
It surely in life is the good stuff!

Murderous

The sickness and brutality,
Why must we continue in this continuity?

Guns, violence, proven guilty,
Prison, sin, and oh so filthy.

Get these guys off the streets,
and defeat their many feats!

Police, yes, I know you've been backlashed,
yet I will respect you until life is cashed.

Policeman, come with me,
Protect and serve us wholeheartedly.

I don't want to be shot, beaten, or raped!
At least not for my sake!

Take these bad guys off the street,
and will win after our bruised society weeps.

Policeman, save me!
From this horrible humanity.

You are here I know
"for the people"
And it shows.

The jury is out,
these bad guys who kill,
Shall be put away,
for life's been shrill!

Killers in the night!
We die from fright!
Let the bad guys be gone,
Let us once again sing in song.

Through It All!

I've been through it all!
Nothing as tall
as getting diagnosed with a mental illness
I thought I'd never fall.

Yes, abused, brokenhearted, and alone
or so I thought
Honey, you hold my life together, so taught.

What can I do but pray
and have faith
that someday,
all this turmoil will go away!

Turn away from the sadness, grief, and frustration,
Come away with, emotion, happiness, and elation.

That's why I give others,
of my time, my love, in every condition.

I want to return to normal,
I can with prescription drugs, informal.

I can't stand being sick!
Before I knew it, it was quick!

They said, "Do you want to be able to take care of your kids?"
I said, "What do you mean? I'm a whiz!"

Genius in a frail, sickened body,
mentally impaired,
yet intellectually there!

How can one stand, the doctors being right?
When all you can think about is the fight!

Please do away with this mental incapacity,
and let me return to sanity.

The pain sets in, it will be a lifelong grin
and bear it forever,
until, forever is no longer, and I win.

Time Does Not Stand Still

Time does not stand still
for no one,
under the sun,
and yet it seems to go on forever, what a pill.

Time giveth and taketh away,
Please, time, stay!

If only we could turn back time,
and rewind.

Maybe then we'll be in business,
or maybe a success.

Oh, thank you, time,
for if not for you, my children would not be mine.

Time, you've given me everything,
and still it is nothing,

To give and to give,
But let me live.

Time, you stand still for no one.
And yet that might not be fun.

We'll wait and see how time affects us,
Cruelly well and yet we don't give a fuss.

To be around you, time,
It is divine.

For you giveth and taketh away,
There is no reason or rhyme.

Time stand still that my family may fill,
my needs and my desires
that I may come out higher.

Out on top of my education and perspiration
Time, you are my motivation.

To beat the clock,
And be in shock.

Of how much we can get done,
In just one day
Time, don't go, stay.

Time, you are a lifeline to my dreams
and yet, time, you cannot be seen!

Time, do me this,
Stop for me.

For this is my phantom wish.

Family

My family
you are so dear to me
You set me free

Without fear,
You hear me

Family, never fail me,
What would I do without my family?

You treat me with kindness and respect,
You suffer with me in all the specks.

The distance you go for me is unknown
But I know, it is the tone,

in which you care,
Oh, family, if I dare,

Care about you in that same way
Oh, will I have to pay?
Family, try me once again,
And I will not fail thee then.

When the going gets tough
and life seems nothing but rough!

Return to greet me in my doorway,
That you might forever stay!

Darkness

Darkness, don't do this to me,
Leave me in the dust, or down an ally.
Darkness, come to me,
For that's when I kneel at my bedside, see.
I don't know how long I've known you but,
Darkness, I owe you.
Some say darkness is terror and fright,
But I say, nah, that's trite.
I like the night.
And in the blackness,
I become a sassafras.
Alone, yes, maybe,
But in my comfort zone, truly.

Someone, speak out!
Oh, I forgot, said no one tout.
The darkness says, come quickly,
I need it, and it needs me.
Darkness, don't shy away,
Come, brighten my holiday.
Without people awake,
I am at peace, and nothing is at stake.
Oh, what a fool I am,
To let darkness dictate where my soul began.
Stay true I say,
Even though the darkness may be at bay.
Sleep tight through the night,
Let darkness guide thy way tonight.

Seasons Change

The seasons change,
the winds rearrange.

The cosmos comes into focus,
it's no longer hocus-pocus.

When will we be through
with this life we once knew?

How do we get by today, tomorrow, and yesteryear?
By holding fast to our dreams, I hear.

I love this land, but it is not all,
That's out there to call.

Home for a time,
And, yes, that was mine.

To see me standing there,
Without a care.

When will my family and friends join me?
And say that they follow on key.

I want to live my life fully,
and not be bullied.

But it's harder than ever now,
because I'm sick and ever so down.

When will my eyes lift up?
And see the Holy One and the Trumps.

Soon enough my child,
until then assume thy style.

And return to me more than,
you ever thought possible.

They took me in

Yes, they took me in,
When I had nowhere to stay
Why did I have to go,
And ruin my flow.

Turns out it was the best thing that ever happened to me
But as you can see,
So happy but without family.

When will they come around?
I am a piece of lost and found!

Why do this to your daughter?
And yet I have a father!

Who I'm sure wanted to see me
Let alone squeeze me freely!

A family from church, the bishop besides,
all by my side.

The home cozy and warm,
Just the place for a teenager to learn.

Come get me, Mother!
And yet prevented by another.

I'm having fun not knowing what I'm missing
Missing all the hugging and kissing.

But held close by these friends,
who comforted me in the end.

They are still there for me!
Cheering me on.

But I missed my brothers,
who are now gone.

Off to college and when will I see them next?
On holidays and such, that is the best.

Why return there, there is no real reason why.
All I do is try, try, try.

And do my best,
To let the rest.

Fall into place,
And find God in that space.

Happiness

Happiness,
You look good on me,
Fleeting, yes, but ever so keen.
Coming to me, you light up the mess.

Happiness, don't flee,
For I know thee
In that space that never lasts,
But for one second, it shall never pass.

Happiness, stay this way forever,
And on that day of pure bliss and splendor,
Be my light, my guide.
And I can be truly happy and joyful inside.

Happiness, come what may.
I choose to bask in your limelight,
And only in that day,
I surely will fight.

For you, Happiness,
You are so chipper
That I don't know anyone more hipper
Than you alone—you are the test.

For me, shall I see you once a day?
Or always in my heart, is where you'll stay?
Be true and steadfast, immovable,
and we shall appreciate happiness inconceivable.

Regret

Oh, Regret!
How we fret!
The lines grow narrow and gray
That we can't see the light of day.

Regret, you move me
But not in a good way.
Please don't stay.
All I can think about is what went wrong!

But then again, I sing with song.
In the end, it can't all be bad.
The things I've learned, it's sad, yes,
But it's what I have.
In my mind, yes, the knowledge was there all along.

Oh, Regret, you have me in a tizzy
That I look around and feel all dizzy.
This can't be! What have I done
To deserve this—not fun!

Regret, oh, this is not working.
You tear me to shreds,
For I am not yet a starling
Who can fly above all the treads.

Oh no, how much longer will this last,
This feeling I get about the past?
Once more, Regret,
I will never forget!

Forgive Me

Father, forgive me for all my misdeeds
And show me the way
That I might fall in your all-loving arms
Every which way every day.

Father, please allow me to see you
For who you are
And what you do for all humanity.
This I know to be true.

Thank thee for the kindness, blessings, and generosity
Shown to me all my days with such veracity.
Let me live for you
And show you what I can do!

Father, you are the one who holds my heart
And pulls me in the right direction from the start.
Please, do I really have to be this true and righteous?
"Yes, my dear, you need to follow me in brightness."

Okay then, what do I have to lose
But the way I should take,
And let me not abuse
Thy love for my sake.

Come to me, Father, in my grief.
Wrap me up in your cloak
Of unimaginable deep
Warmth surrounding me.

Oh, when will I see thee again?
Father, forgive me.
And that is when?
Love me until the end!

About the Author

The author's name is Kimberly Dorough. She is married with two children, a boy and a girl. She is a nurse, volunteers at her children's schools for their events, and rescues animals and also pet-sits. She loves to create blankets with her sewing machine for anybody and everybody. She also crotchets. She enjoys spending time with her family, feeding the missionaries from their church, organizing, and decorating. She loves the fall, Halloween, Thanksgiving, Christmas, and New Year's! She reads music and plays the flute and piano. She also loves to ice-skate when time allows. She loves taking pictures and scrapbooking and also loves doing family history.